JaimePacheco

March 1, 1942 – May 25, 1972

COVER PHOTO: Doug Sterner (foreground) providing cover fire for the radioman in the background, Jaime Pacheco. This photo, taken on one of the author's last missions with Ranger Team 75 has become one of the most recognized pictures of the Vietnam War.

Jaime's Story
God Is Good

A true story of friendship and Faith.

By C. Douglas Sterner

A Son's Tribute to His Father

I never really had the chance to meet my father. I was only 18 months old when he was killed in Vietnam. Throughout my life I often wondered about him, what kind of man he was, how he lived and died. I didn't know that for 25 years my father's closest friend had been looking for me, anticipating my questions, anxious to share the answers with me. Publication of the cover photo on this booklet on the cover of the 1997 1st Cavalry Division calendar set in motion a chain of events that finally brought Doug Sterner and I together.

When we talked for the first time on January 20, 1998, my first words were, "What can you tell me about my father." That night he faxed me the pages of a small booklet he wrote in 1973 shortly after my father was killed in action, a booklet he had never published but had kept along with my father's letters to him throughout the years. This booklet told me more about my father than I could have hoped for. I am happy to share it with you here in honor of the hero I never really met, my father, Jaime Pacheco.

Michael Pacheco

Dedicated To:

MICHAEL & TYLER PACHECO-VEHAR

*The Son & Grandson of a Great Man
and Wonderful Christian Warrior*

JAIME PACHECO-VEHAR

Jaime in Vietnam (1971 – 1972)

PREFACE

Life is often measured in terms of months, decades, and years. For the young soldier facing combat on foreign shores life can be defined.... and lost....in fleeting seconds. In one moment of horror a bond was born between Jaime Pacheco and I in Vietnam, a bond that would impact my life forever. In yet another fleeting second, Jaime lost his life.

This booklet was written six months after Jaime was killed in Vietnam. I never really intended it for publication and perhaps thought of it more as a personal diary or journal. The single copy I made in 1973 remained stored away for 25 years with my black beret, Jaime's letters, the letter from our Ranger Executive Officer detailing Jaime's death, and a letter from Jaime's wife (written to me a month after Jaime died.) Through the years and several moves, all of my photos and other physical memorabilia from two tours in Vietnam were lost. Only the aforementioned survived the quarter century.

Of all the photos, copies of news stories I had written, and other personal memorabilia; the one item I lamented the loss of most was a picture taken of Jaime and me shortly after the mission referred to in this booklet. Through the years, however, I found I did not need a photograph to keep Jaime constantly in memory. As an active public speaker much involved in veteran's programs, I talked of Jaime often. Throughout the years there was seldom a night that I did not wonder where Michael Pacheco, the boy who was only 18 months old when his father was killed, was. Growing up my four children knew both Michael and Jaime by name, though they had never met. My reoccurring dream was that one day I would visit Jaime's grave in Hobbs, New Mexico, and while standing there, would finally meet his family.

Of the thousands of photographs in the historical files of the First Cavalry Division, the fact that the picture of Jaime and me that meant so much would one day be "randomly" chosen and published on the cover of the official *Cav Calendar*, is beyond coincidence. I should not have been surprised, for it seems God has interwoven Jaime's and my life from the moment we first met. With the publication of the calendar I felt a renewed urgency to find Jaime's family and share the calendar with them.

On January 20, 1998, a year after the calendar was published, I received a long distance call from Texas from a young lady identifying herself as Lenay Pacheco, Michael Pacheco's wife. After all the years, all the wrong phone calls and lost letters, thanks to the staff at Angel Fire, New Mexico, Jaime's son and I would finally meet.

The phone conversation that evening was long and emotional, but a dream come true. Michael asked, "What can you tell me about my father?" For the first time in more than 20 years I pulled this booklet from my files and reread it. When I finished I felt that it said more about Jaime and who he was than anything I could say over the phone. That same evening I faxed a copy to Michael. The following day, after making photocopies for myself, I sent him the originals of Jaime's letters, written in his father's own hand twenty-five years before.

Within a month I was contacted by Jaime's sister, and shortly thereafter spoke with Jaime's mother by phone. I shared with them copies of the calendar, and Michael shared with them copies of my fax to him containing this story. At their request I am sharing it herein. It is almost without exception, word-for-word as I wrote it months after Jaime's death.

As I speak and visit with veterans groups around the country, I am constantly amazed at how the friendships forged in battle often become lifetime associations. The friendship Jaime and I shared was not only forged in battle, it was nurtured by God. Though Jaime is gone, the impact of his life on mine has survived not only the test of time, but his own death. In many ways when I speak, write, or serve our Nation in any capacity; I like to believe that a part of Jaime Pacheco lives on in me.

C. Douglas Sterner
21 May 1998

Footnote to the Preface

On Memorial Day, May 25, 1998... **26 years to the day after Jaime's death**...I met Jaime's family. As Michael and I went through his father's personal effects he handed me a box containing a Bible. As I held it in my hands, for the first time in 26 years, I opened it and read the inscription:

"To Jaime Pacheco, From Doug Sterner, 15 March 1972."

That same Memorial Day, wearing the original beret presented to me on behalf of Ranger Team 75 by my closest friend, I held Jaime's mother in my arms as she introduced me as her "oldest son". At the close of Memorial Day Services in Angel Fire, NM I was overwhelmed by emotion as I watched my 21 year old daughter join hands with the 28 year old son of Jaime Pacheco on the platform of the Vietnam Memorial to sing "God Bless America".

Today my best friend's son calls me "dad", and though I know I can never replace the father he lost, I have made the commitment to become the father he found. Somewhere above I believe Jaime is looking down at me with a smile on his face and saying, "Doug, you were a true brother.

"GOD IS GOOD!"

The author, Jaime's mother and Michael Pacheco meeting for the first time on Memorial Day, 25 May 1998 at Angel Fire, NM/

3

The Sterner family meeting and adopting Michael Pacheco at Angel Fire, New Mexico, 26 years to the day after his father was killed in Vietnam.

One month after meet the Sterners and talking openly for the first time about the death of his father, Michael took his wife Lenay and son Tyler for their first ever visit to the Traveling Vietnam Wall..

CONTACT!

A trickle of sweat began to inch down my forehead and sting in my eyes as I struggled through the thick brush. The heavy pack crushed my back and the straps cut through my shoulders. Despite the shade of the dense jungle foliage, the heat was stifling and seemed to burn through my whole body. I put a hand to my face to brush away another bead of perspiration and it came away covered with the green stain of camouflage face paint I was wearing.

My back still burned like a thousand tiny needles were piercing the skin, the grim reminder of the consequences of stumbling over a red ant pile. There was an irritating pain in one leg and I knew at least one leach had "hitched a ride" as I'd crept along. Ahead, a ray of sunlight was breaking through the brush indicating we were near a clearing. Knowing how dangerous it could be to cross an open area, I gripped my CAR-15 rifle more tightly in my sweaty hands. A branch hit me in the face making a scratch that soon stung with the salty burn of sweat. "Nineteen more days and I will be home," I thought silently. "Home....away from Vietnam, away from the jungle, away from the heat, the leaches, the red ants, and yes, away from the war.

My thoughts were interrupted when Stubby, the man ahead of me, turned and whispered one word..."Dinks", our slang term for the enemy. Instantly I froze, my eyes scanning the trail we were breaking out on. Another trickle of sweat rolled down the tip of my nose and I suppressed an urge to brush it aside. My heart was pounding like a drum but around me all was quiet. Too quiet! It was uncanny. "Nineteen days, " I thought again.

"What am I doing here?"

Suddenly there was the sharp, staccato beat of automatic rifle fire. There was no time to think now. I threw my pack to the ground hanging on to my rifle and my camera. I hit the edge of the clearing at a run and flung myself to the ground behind a mound of dirt, my CAR-15 rifle spitting flame and lead almost before I felt the hot dust beneath me.

"Xray, Xray, this is 75, 75...Contact, Contact, Contact," I could hear our radio man Specialist Four Jaime Pacheco yell into the radio.

"How many were out there?" I wondered. There were only seven of us, a mere handful of men. Then came the dull roar of a detonating hand grenade and a cloud of smoke and dust rolled over my position. "I must have been crazy," I said to myself as I kicked an empty magazine out of my weapon and inserted another 30-round clip. Then I had to laugh a little under my breath. "Me, crazy?" That was just what everyone else had been calling me.

For a year and a half my friends had called me crazy for the foolish bravado I exhibited. When I arrived in Vietnam it was to work in the capacity of a combat engineer, which I did through two tours. Three months before my second tour was to end I was transferred to the 3rd Brigade, 1st Air Cavalry Division where I managed to con my way into a job as a combat correspondent for the military news media. Action in Vietnam was winding down, and this new role allowed me to go wherever the action might be.

Because my tour was nearing its completion I'd been informed by my superiors that I would not be allowed to go "in the field" for my stories, but would work in the office and around our base camp at Bien Hoa. I was not one to sit behind a desk for long, however, and was even worse at following orders. I started making trips to the jungle against orders "bouncing with the Blues", our quick reaction force, on several missions. Our commanding officer would review my stories and photos, shake his head, and forbid further excursions. "You're too short (our slang term for having a short time left in our combat tour) to be going in the field," he would say. "I don't want o have to write your parents and tell them, 'I know Sergeant Sterner was supposed to be home in a couple of weeks but.....'."

His protests aside, he continued to publish my stories and photos in he unit newspaper. I kept returning to the jungle for more. I enjoyed the freedom of going out with different units and being where the action was, out before my tour ended there was one story I was determined to get the one story I was sure would be an exclusive.

For years our office had tried to get a correspondent on a mission with a team from H Troop, 75th Rangers. All efforts had failed, not so much because Rangers were publicity shy, but because the nature of their mission was so unique that an untrained man could mean disaster. These men, who wore the much envied black beret, were an elite unit that hunted the enemy in the most silent and deadly fashion. Working in teams of five or six men, they were famed for their occasional reconnaissance missions. Their most common mission however, was what they called "hunter-killer" missions, operations where they stalked the enemy with stealth and skill using highly honed guerrilla tactics to out-maneuver and ultimately destroy him.

After more than a year of unsuccessful attempts to write and photograph the Cav's rangers in action, our public information office had given up on the possibility of getting that story. I wasn't satisfied and boasted that before my tour ended, I would it. My superiors in turn told me that even if the Ranger Company gave their consent (in itself considered an impossibility), they would not allow me to take the job. Normally any man with less than 30 days "in country" was kept on the base camp. I had been consistently in the jungle right up through the Tet holiday just four weeks before my scheduled return home.

Then, miraculously, the Ranger commander agreed to let me accompany a team on a mission. No one in our office could understand the change in his attitude, and not until later did I understand the reason. At the time, some of the men in our office believed that it was my persistence and military record over two tours that had persuaded the Rangers to take me on, I know now that God had a plan behind it all.

"Sergeant Sterner," my senior NCO said just before I left on my first of several missions with Ranger Team 75, "You really are crazy!" And then I was one my way--my last mission in Vietnam and the chance to get my exclusive story.

Actually, I would eventually pull several missions with the team in the short time remaining in my tour. My first lasted only a few hours. The chopper inserted the seven-man team just before noon and at four in the afternoon we walked within ten feet of an enemy soldier hidden in the dense jungle. When the firing subsided we were extracted and flown back to Bien Hoa for the night. The following morning we were inserted again in another area. So here I was, two contacts in two days, and my tour of duty was almost over. I knew I had to make this one good.

Remembering what my job here was, I jumped to my feet and snapped a picture. In that brief instant I saw a flicker of flame. One of our grenades had started a brush fire. Before I could move Jaime was rushing forward at a crouch to beat out the flames. I snapped another picture, then sent a burst of fire from my weapon to cover Jaime's return to his position.

Overhead I heard the beat of helicopter blades slicing the air above the trees. Our team leader was barking instructions into Jaime's radio, "We have movement to the south, about a hundred yards out." Then came the crash of rockets and the scream of a Cobra gunship making its lethal dive. Another grenade thundered and I slapped a fresh magazine in my weapon and continued to fire. And then silence came. The enemy had withdrawn and the fight was over....for me at least.

The team leader jerked his head my way. "Sterner, cover the trail for the radio man," he said matter-of-factly, treating me as a member of the team and not just a correspondent who was along for the trip. I responded by moving to the center of the trail and taking up a defensive position while a reconnaissance element went out to check our "kill zone".

The recon team found a bunker complex and was gone for some time. Then came the sound of a grenade and Jaime turned and said, "I hope that was one of ours." I nodded grimly and, suddenly realizing how thirsty I was, got out my canteen and took a long drink. I offered it to Jaime and between the two of us it was quickly drained. Still thirsty, we made short

8

work of Jaime's canteen, and then went to work on the five-quart flask in his back.

As we waited for the recon element to return we had time to talk and snap a few more pictures to send home. We were two soldiers who had just survived a moment of danger together, and that puts a unique bond between men. Such bonds were not uncommon among the soldiers who fought in Vietnam, but soon Jaime and I would find an even stronger bond, one that would tie our lives together for eternity.

10

AMIGO, ASTA LEUGO!

It was Sunday night and as usual I was at our chapel for the Sunday evening service, the only one of its kind in our unit. It was a very informal service consisting of lively singing, personal testimonies, and group sharing. We were singing when I heard someone coming in late and turned in time to see Jaime take a seat near the back of the chapel. He caught my eye and nodded and I acknowledged his presence with a similar silent nod of the head. This was Jaime's first visit to our chapel service, and knowing he was Catholic I was somewhat surprised to see him visit our less orthodox Protestant worship session.

When the service concluded I invited Jaime to stick around and visit over a cold soda. As we walked to a group of my friends in a corner of the chapel I told him, "It sure is good to see you here, Jaime." It had only be a few days since I had pulled my last mission with Team 75.

Following completion of my required five missions (I actually went on a sixth just seven days before my tour was to end), the team initiated me as a member of the unit, a Ranger tradition. I was promised a beret in the coming days, though I neglected in my efforts to prepare for my departure, to get one. Instead, I wrote my story, made copies of all the pictures I had taken for the men of the team to send home, and was busily getting my affairs in order to leave Vietnam the following week.

"It's good to be here," Jaime replied with a smile, and I knew he sincerely meant it. "You know something Doug," he continued, "It is kind of funny the way we met. I knew the first time I saw you that you were a Christian and God had sent you out with our team just so you and I could meet."

Now I smiled. "Yes Jaime, that is the way God is. He works out all these things with some master plan we may not understand, but it all has a reason. I wouldn't want to be here and not be a Christian. It really is a good life."

"It sure is Doug. Boy, I'll tell you something, God is sure good!" And that was the first time I heard Jaime mention the phrase that I now associate with him in every fond remembrance.

The following evening I was again at the chapel, this time to practice some music with "*The King's Children*", a gospel singing group I had started on the base a few months earlier. We were singing a Bill Gaither song titled "Jesus, There's Just Something About That Name" when I noticed Jaime come in and again take a seat at the back of the chapel. As we sang I saw a noticeable glow in his eyes, and when we finished he looked up quietly and said, "I hope I'm not interrupting anything, but that is the most beautiful song I have ever heard. Would you sing it again for me?" We did, and as we sang one couldn't miss the tears that formed in Jaime's eyes. I couldn't help but think, "There sat a man deeply in love with Jesus Christ."

Several times that week Jaime returned to listen to us as we practiced, and always he would ask us to sing that same song over and over again. It became his favorite, as well as ours.

Often during that week Jaime and I would talk late into the night. He had many questions about the Bible, about Jesus, and about living the Christian life. In that week we became close, very close. For me it was a new experience for I had always been somewhat of a loner who avoided close ties to others in Vietnam. But in that last week a bond of brotherly love grew between us that I shall never understand or forget.

Jaime also spoke often of his family back home, and especially his wife and small son. He informed me that his wife made "the best Mexican food you have ever ate and will ever eat. A Big Brag but it can be kept." We made a pact that, when Jaime finally returned to the United States I would come and visit his home in Hobbs, New Mexico, meet his family, and test his brag about his wife's cooking.

Mid-week came and on Wednesday Jaime left on a mission with his team. I hoped and prayed he would get back before I left for home as I was scheduled to depart the following Monday. Sunday arrived all too quickly but I was thrilled to see Jaime walk into the chapel service that evening. He took a seat beside me in the front and together we sang, we prayed together and we worshipped God.

When the service concluded we gathered again at the rear of the chapel to visit. I spent a good deal of time saying "good-by" to my friends before they returned to their barracks. When everyone else was gone I urned to Jaime and said, "I have to stop by the office tonight, so I can walk hat far with you on your way back to the Ranger compound."

We stepped outside the chapel and the beauty of the night was enough to warm the heart. The sky was clear with a scattering of stars and a bright moon. The air was warm with a breeze that was refreshing but not too hot or too cold. I was struck by the magnificence of God's creation, even in a war zone. "Thank you God", I thought silently, "for beautiful nights like this, and for the kind of friendship You have given me and Jaime."

As we walked we talked again of family and friends, but mostly about Jesus. There was a real sadness in parting but it was also a time of joy in the realization that, when the bond of Christian love exists, you are never far separated.

Then we reached the door to the Public Information Office where I was to clean out the last of my personal effects. We paused for a long moment of silence, neither of us wanting to say goodbye. For a moment I felt guilty. For months I had tried to extend for yet a third tour in Vietnam and been denied each time. I wanted to stay in Vietnam and was being sent home against my wishes.

Jaime had a wife and young son. He not only wanted to be home, he needed to be home. I wished that somehow we could trade places, even wondered if I was deserting my friends by leaving. It was an emotion-packed, awkward time of silence, with neither of us wanting to say goodbye.

Then Jaime looked at me and smiled. "You know Doug, God is good." I smiled again at his classic statement. "We won't say goodbye, for we'll meet again someday, somewhere."

"Yes, Jaime," I replied fighting back a rush of tears, "we'll meet again. Just as soon as you are back in the States I'll be knocking on your door, just waiting to try your wife's cooking."

"Doug?"

"Yes Jaime?"

"Whatever happens, God IS good!"

"Yes Jaime, He sure is."

"I better be going Doug. Amigo, Asta Leugo."

And then he was gone, walking away into the night. The tears came as I watched him leave. And then, just before he disappeared from view I experienced a strange feeling.

I knew that I was looking at Jaime Pacheco for the last time.

IN CHRIST – YOUR BROTHER

Before I'd left Vietnam I'd learned from Jaime that he did not own a Bible. My first concern upon my arrival home was to purchase one. I had his name embossed on the cover and mailed it to him along with several religious paperback books. A few weeks later I got my first letter in reply.

When I'd been with Ranger Team 75, after my initiation, I'd been promised their coveted black Ranger beret. The team had kept their promise to award me one and asked Jaime to mail it to me. In fact, Jaime opted to send me his own, well-worn beret. It is one of the very few mementos of my Vietnam service that I still have, and it is indeed the one that means the most to me.

In his letter Jaime talked mostly about how good God was and how much it meant to him to be a Christian. There was some talk about the team and how things were going in the "bush", mention of family and home, and repeated mention of how much he enjoyed his new Bible and other books. The letter closed with four words that became my friend's standard closing: "In Christ, Your Brother, Jaime Pacheco."

A few weeks later another letter came. "I don't know what our good Lord has for me," Jaime wrote, "but I tell you, when He leads or shows me to where He wants me I'll know I can't ever be happy unless I do as He wants me to. As for my going home, I don't know yet. I'll just let Him take care of that as He has taken care of me in ALL things."

I read and wept unashamed at his simple faith in God and the way he unreservedly committed his entire life and future into God's hands. Before he closed with "Your fellow Brother in Christ," Jaime wrote, "I know if it be Our Lord's will to go back to the States alive and well, we, my family and I will meet again some day."

Every night I would lay in my bed back home and pray that God would keep His hand on Jaime, would keep him safe and free from harm,

15

and bring him safely home soon. I waited eagerly for each letter, and the third arrived shortly after Jaime had written it. It was dated 12 May 1972.

By this time Jaime knew that it would be some time before he would be coming home. As a Ranger he was much in demand and the rash of troop withdrawals would not affect him. "Man let me tell you," he wrote, "I am ready to go home right now! Personally I would, like I said, go home right now, but if I had my way I would like to go the 15th of June so I could be there for her (his wife's) birthday, and after all out processing, arrive at my home town the morning of the 20th of June. But the way things look it seems that it will be more like in August or the very latest, October. But at any rate, I am going to let God lead me and use me according to His will. Yes, that is the way to be Doug, God IS GOOD."

He closed the letter as my brother in Christ as was his usual pattern. In this letter there was a slight change in the closing lines, however, it would be two months before I was to notice it or understand what it meant.

I continued to pray for Jaime, asking God to protect him. Every day I would check the mail which came to my father's house in Montana, in hopes there would be another letter. In the previous weeks Jaime had been asking me to tape some Gospel music to send him. I had been singing with friends in a neighboring town, and every time we got together to sing I thought of my promise to send Jaime some music. Somehow, we just never seemed to get it done. I was thinking about this as I drove home from work one day early in June. I would be visiting my singing friends that very weekend and resolved that whatever it took, I was going to get Jaime's tape made.

As I passed my father's house on the way to my apartment, I stopped to check the mail. There was one letter. It was from the Department of the Army. My hands trembled as I opened it, knowing deep inside what it was going to say. The black type blurred beneath a rush of tears. I struggled to believe it said something else. But no, there it was in black and white:

"I regret to inform you that Specialist Pacheco died on 25 May, 1972."

GOD IS GOOD

"God, NO!" I cried in anguish. As I struggled to drive home, my vision was blurred by tears. I couldn't help repeatedly asking, out loud, "God, WHY?"

Then bitterness started to creep in.

"God is good," Jaime had written just 13 days before his death. Somehow I now felt it hard to accept that fact. How could a good God allow something like this to happen? Of all the people, why Jaime?

Throughout the sleepless night the question arose again and again, "God, why?" And then came my own feelings of guilt, guilt that I had survived and anger at myself for being safe at home while my best friend died.

"What if I had been there?" I wondered. Could my being with Jaime in that moment of danger have changed the outcome somehow?" I'd lost many friends in Vietnam including a platoon leader I had greatly admired, but somehow this struck a nerve that wouldn't heal. Of all the people, why Jaime? It just didn't seem fair. Where was God?

A few weeks later a letter arrived from the executive officer of the Ranger detachment detailing for me how Jaime had died. Jaime had been covering the rear of a recon element that walked into an enemy bunker complex. As the firefight ensued Jaime realized the danger that threatened the three men ahead of him. Leaving his more secure area at the rear of the team he rushed forward firing his weapon and throwing more than a dozen grenades, permitting his comrades to safely withdraw. Then, as the team pulled back, a round from a malfunctioning helicopter minigun struck him and took his life.

For his heroic actions that day, Jaime was awarded the Silver Star Medal. But the point that stood out far above his heroic actions was the love for his comrades that compelled him to risk his life so that they might live. It was characteristic of the Jesus Jaime loved so much, He Who once said,

17

"Greater love hath no man that this, that a man lay down his life for his friends."

Of Jaime Pacheco, the Ranger executive officer wrote: "I can honestly say that he is one of the few in this world who had no enemies."

Still I couldn't help wondering, and questioning God.

The following Sunday I attended church with a mixture of anger and puzzlement in God's failure to protect my friend. The choir stood to sing and the song was Jaime's favorite, "Jesus, There's Just Something About that name". Again I could not restrain the tears.

A letter from Jaime's widow followed. It was one filled with both sorrow and faith. "Yes, 'God is Good'," Olga Pacheco wrote. "It is my wish and prayer that the 'Good God' continue helping me face my future with a smile, a smile at God in loving acceptance of whatever He sends into my life now, so that I may merit to have the radiant, smiling face of Christ gaze on me for all eternity."

Still I wept long and bitter tears. For two months I mourned and questioned, wondered and wept. Few had been the acquaintances that I had ever allowed to become so close, and despite my puzzlement at how God could have allowed Jaime to die, I knew deep inside that the bond that had grown between us had been nurtured by God for some unknown reason in His master plan.

Once again I picked up Jaime's last letter to me and read it as I had so many times in the previous weeks. It was so bright and characteristic of Jaime's simple faith, and as I read I could almost picture the light in Jaime's eyes and the smile that was so uniquely characteristic of him. I read his words again, "That is the way to be Doug, God IS Good." I found the statement a little hard to accept now that Jaime was gone. At the letter's end he had written, "Amigo, Asta Luego," and I remembered the warm night in Vietnam just scant months earlier when we had parted with those words and Jaime had vanished into the darkness.

Finally I reached his closing line and signature, "In CHRIST Your Brother...." but wait, there was something sandwiched between the words in CAPITAL letters, something I had never noticed before. In the letter Jaime wrote me just 13 days before sacrificed his life for his friends, he closed with the words "In CHRIST, FOR ETERNITY, Your Brother, Jaime Pacheco."

18

For the first time a warm glow filled my heart and a smile came to my face in the sweet, powerful realization of what Jaime had told me in that final goodbye. Somehow he sensed he was not going to be coming home; that he would die in Vietnam.   He also knew he was prepared for that moment. It wasn't really goodbye after all. "In CHRIST, FOR ETERNITY, Your Brother...."

"Yes my Jaime," I said aloud to myself,

"GOD IS GOOD!"

RANGER STORY

This story was first published as text for a photo lay-out in the Garry Owen newspaper and the First Team Magazine in March 1972 after my missions with Ranger Team 75. The cover photo as well as other photos in this booklet were official US ARMY PHOTOS from that story layout.)

Silence Is Their Only Advantage

On a Mission
With Team 75

EDITOR'S NOTE: Little has been said or written of the Rangers in Vietnam, the teams of men who creep through the jungle living the proverbial "life of danger," seeking out the enemy in a silent and deadly fashion and meeting him with the same terms and tactics he has employed against us. It isn't that Rangers are publicity shy, but to effectively tell their story one must live with them, hump with them, and fight with them. Seldom is the privilege of sharing their lives extended to a correspondent, or for that matter, any outsider. The Ranger Team is an elite team, specially trained to do a special job, and an untrained man can mean disaster. Though many units claim to be Ranger, there actually is only one Ranger unit currently conducting operations in Vietnam. That is H Company, 75th Rangers, descendants of the 5307th Composite Unit (Merrill's Marauders) of World War II fame. The tales of their exploits in the jungles of Southeast Asia are nothing less than spectacular. Recently Ranger Team 75

agreed to allow SGT Doug Sterner to accompany them on a mission. This is SGT Sterner's account of his mission with the team.

By SGT Doug Sterner

The Huey "slick" hardly seemed to stop in its descent on the clearing before Ranger Team 75 was on the ground and moving rapidly to the edge of the jungle. As I lunged through the underbrush I glanced back long enough to see our rear scout, SP4 Kenneth (Snuffy) Anderson backing out of the clearing in a crouch, ready for any signs of the enemy. I wanted desperately to stop to shoot a picture, but now wasn't the time. We had to get to cover before the enemy had a chance to locate us. The pictures would have to wait. Once the team was concealed in the brush, SGT Paul "Blinky" Morguez, the Team Leader (TL) for 75, motioned to us to sit down. It was a relief to drop my heavy pack and relax in the brush. Somewhere a

bird began to sing, and it was almost like being back in Montana. All was so quiet and peaceful it was almost possible to forget that you were hiding in enemy-infested jungle, just a handful of men and their weapons.

CPL Jairus Pacheco, RTO for the team, unsheathed his radio. When the TL began to make his report to the rear he spoke only in a whisper. No one made a noise. Quietly, I unsnapped my camera, focused it, and pushed the button to release the shutter. It sounded like a bomb dropping in a soundproof room, and everyone turned quickly to look at me. A little embarrassed, I put up my camera and resolved my pictures would have to wait a little longer.

After about 20 minutes the TL felt assured that the enemy had not noticed our insertion and had not come in our direction. We hitched up our rucks, and began moving through the brush. There were no trails, no paths; we just walked and crawled where we could, never making a sound. No one spoke, not one

The huey "Slick" hardly seemed to stop in its descent on the clearing before Ranger Team 75 was on the ground and moving rapidly to the edge of the jungle. As I lunged through the underbrush I glanced back long enough to see our rear scout, Sp4 Kenneth (Snuffy) Anderson backing out of the clearing in a crouch, ready for any signs of the enemy. I wanted desperately to stop for a chance to shoot a picture, but now wasn't the time. We had to get to cover before the enemy had a chance to locate us. The pictures would have to wait.

Once the team was concealed in the brush, Sgt Paul "Blinky" Morguez, Team Leader (TL) for 75 motioned for us to sit down. It was a relief to drop my heavy pack and relax in the brush. Some where a bird began to sing, and it was almost possible to forget that you were hiding in enemy infested jungle, just a handful of men and their weapons.

Sp4 Jaime Pacheco, RTO for the team, unsheathed his radio. When the TL began to make his report to the rear he spoke only in a whisper. No one made any noise. Quietly I unsnapped my camera, focused it, and pushed the button to release the shutter. It sounded like a bomb dropping in a sound proof room and everyone turned quickly to look at me. A little embarrassed, I put my camera up and resolved that my pictures would have to wait a little longer.

After about 20 minutes the TL felt confident that the enemy had not noticed our insertion and had not come in our direction. We hitched up our rucks and began moving through the brush. There were no trails, no paths, we just walked and crawled where we could, never making a sound. No one spoke, not one vine was cut from our path, and so well hidden was each man by the heavy brush and camouflage jungle fatigues and face paint that often I would lose sight of "Stubby", Sgt Lynn Morrison, who was walking just ahead of me.

My ruck was beginning to give me pains and sweat poured off me. It was rough on me, and try as I might to hide it, anyone could see I was tired. I started glancing at the other members to see how they were taking it. They were sweating too, which made me feel a little better. That is, all except "Blinky" who I was sure by now could out walk a horse. Someone once said that Rangers don't have to shoot the enemy, they just hump them to death. I was beginning to believe this was the truth.

There were times I wished I had packed a little more, though my ruck was more than heavy enough for me. But a five-day log of supplies to a Ranger seemed awful meager to me. Three LRRP meals won't last the average grunt a day and a half, and I was expected to make them last for five days. And six quarts of water, a two day supply for most grunts, had to be stretched out over that same five day period.

Finally we paused for a few minutes. It was getting well along into the afternoon and the heat seemed to be reaching extremes. I lifted my canteen to my lips, rationing myself the barest amount of water, and settled back to listen. There was a crackling of brush that made my heart beat a little faster. I strained my eyes and saw two chickens strutting about. They walked within 20 feet of me but so quiet was the team that they never realized we were in the area.

Twenty minutes later we were moving on again. We were reaching an open area and "Stubby" stopped beside me. "When we cross this area," he said, "make sure you step on the branches and not on the ground." It seemed strange to me, but Stubby explained that in the open area if the enemy were near they would see us, so the sound of a breaking twig made little difference. Now the important thing was to insure that we left no footprints for the enemy to find. Later Sp4 Pacheco explained that the Team tries to leave no evidence of its presence after it has passed. "We even eat the plastic containers our LRRPs come in so the enemy can't find them," he said with a laugh.

We finally stopped in a small clearing and I decided to chance a few more pictures. Muffling my camera as best I could with my towel, I took a few shots, then helped myself to a drink from my canteen. We'd been in the jungle for about four hours and yet my canteen was practically full. It was surprising.

It was getting dark as we moved on, though it was still early in the evening. Then the Team stopped. Blinky was on the point and had broken onto a trail. While we waited he scouted the trail with Sp4 Melvin Mullis, the assistant TL who had been walking "slack". Then they motioned for the team to move up. I was just breaking through the under- growth when the world exploded. Dropping to the ground I worked out of my ruck and alternated between shooting pictures of the elite team in action, and talking back to the hidden enemy with my AR-15 rifle.

For Blinky it had been close. Breaking from the trail and into the open, he had heard a man to his left shout at him in Vietnamese. The enemy soldier had undoubtedly mistaken us for NVA or VC troops. He had been no more than 10 feet from Blinky when he spoke, and the TL had answered with a burst from his AR-15.

"Make sure you cover our rear," I heard Blinky yell, and then from back on the trail I heard Snuffy yell back, "Yeah, I've got it."

"Frag out," yelled 1Lt Lynn Moore, the Ranger operations officer who was along for the trip. As he stood to throw his grenade the team covered with a burst of fire.

"Someone pass me a cigarette," yelled Blinky, crouching now and firing from the hip.

Then Pacheco, talking into the mouthpiece of the radio, "Xray, Xray, 75, 75. Contact! Contact! Contact!"

Then all was quiet again save for the sound of Blue Max (our helicopter gunships) waiting overhead. Blinky took two men and scouted the area where the enemy had been. All that could be found was a thick trail

23

through the brush where he had "duffed". Pacheco and I sat back drawing long gulps on our canteens. We could drink all we wanted now. We had a contact and would be pulled out.

When all was clear we moved into the open and popped smoke for our bird. While the skids were still well above the ground I felt the other members of the team boosting me in. Then I turned to haul them aboard. The door gunners opened fire on the area and we left with tracers tearing the brush in case any enemy had followed us to the PZ. As the chopper circled we could see Max diving in on the position we had just left, tearing the jungle with his rockets and minigun. We were on our way back to the rear for a hot meal, a cold soda, a shower and a good night's sleep. My job was finished but for Team 75 there would be tomor-row...another day, another mission, and perhaps another contact.

A drink of water helps break the jungle heat (right). Later, Ranger Team 75 waits for extraction after completion of its mission.

Sterner   Sterner

There were TWO versons to the details of Jaime's death:

The Offical Version	The Way it Happened
This version was related in his Silver Star citation. It was the only version ever to to his family.	Jamie's family was unaware of these details for 26 years. Learning the truth brought closure to many nagging doubts they held for years.

Those who do not understand the nature of warfare will find in these conflicting accounts reason to condemn the military. I neither condone nor condemn the decision not to tell the family all the details, I simply UNDERSTAND.

APPENDIXES

❖ **Jaime's Silver Star Citation**
❖ **Letter from H Troop detailing Jaime's Death**
❖ **Jaime's letter to me dated 16 April 1972**
❖ **Jaime's letter to me dated 12 May 1972**
❖ **Olga Pacheco's letter to me dated 1 July 1972**
❖ **Epilogue**

When I met Jaime's family for the first time on Memorial Day 1998, I prepared a dozen copies of the previously unpublished "Jaime's Story" to give each member of the family. At the Pacheco-Vejar family reunion in June 2002 the family inquired if I could make additional copies available, which I was happy to do.

In the earlier printing I included ONLY the text of the story. In this new edition, at the request of Jaime's family, I am including Jaime's last letters to me. I have neither edited them or corrected them for spelling, but included them herein as close as possible to the way they were originally written. Emphasized text and underlines are used ONLY where Jaime himself emphasized or underlined words in his letters.

DEPARTMENT OF THE ARMY
Headquarters, U S Army/Vietnam/MACV Support Command
APO San Francisco 96375

19 August 1972
GENERAL ORDERS
NUMBER 1923
AWARD OF THE SILVER STAR
TC 439. The following AWARD is announced posthumously.
PACHECO, JAIME SPECIALIST FOUR U.S. Army, Company H (Ranger),

75th Infantry, 3d Brigade (Separate), 1st Cavalry Division, APO 96490

Awarded: Silver Star
Date of action: 25 May 1972
Theater: Republic of Vietnam
Authority: By direction of the President, under the provisions of the
Act of Congress, approved 9 July 1918.
REASON:

For gallantry in action while engaged in military operations involving conflict
with an armed hostile force in the Republic of Vietnam: Specialist Four
Pacheco distinguished himself on 25 May 1972 while serving as medic on a
Ranger Team which was on a reconnaissance mission in Tan Uyen
Province, Republic of Vietnam. Specialist Pacheco walked as rear scout for
a four man point reconnaissance element when the element discovered an
enemy bunker complex. As the first three men of the element exhausted
their first magazines, Specialist Pacheco immediately recognized the
danger caused by the lull in firing and rushed the bunkers firing his own
weapon and throwing fragmentation grenades. As the team withdrew from
the bunker complex, he remained in his position and continued to throw a
total of twelve fragmentation grenades, covering the team's withdrawal. By
holding the enemy at bay his fellow soldiers were able to escape without
injury. When he attempted to rejoin his team, he was hit by enemy fire
which wounded him fatally. His actions gave the team the precious time
they needed to reach safety. Specialist Pacheco's gallantry in action and
devotion to duty, at the cost of his life, were in keeping with the highest
traditions of the military service and reflect great credit upon himself, his
unit and the United States Army.

FOR THE COMMANDER:
HAROLD H. DUNWOODY
Brigadier General, US Army
Acting Chief of Staff

26

DEPARTMENT OF THE ARMY
Company H (Ranger) 75th Infantry (Airborne)
Task Force "Garry Owen" Provinscial
1st Cavalry Division (Airmobile)

5 July 1972

Mr. C. Doug Sterner
Route 48
Anaconda, Montana

Dear Sir:

SP/4 Jaime Pacheco was killed in action on 25 May 1972, while serving as Team medic for Ranger Team 76 which was on a reconnaissance mission approximately 10 kilometers north of fire support base Spudis. Walking in the position of rear scout, SP/4 Pacheco accompanied a point reconnaissance element which walked into a bunker complex. As the lead element made contact and expended its initial magazine, a dangerous lull in fireing (sic) ensued. Realizing the danger, SP/4 Pacheco rushed forward and covered the withdrawal of the point reconnaissance by fireing (sic) his own weapon and throwing 12-15 fragmentation grenades. (Because this action allowed the entire element to withdraw unharmed and because it showed great valor with little concern for his own safety SP/4 Pacheco has been submitted for a Silver Star). Once contact had been broken, the point reconnaissance returned to the rest of the team, and the Team Leader requested a pink team and a section of Max gunships. The Team Leader worked out the pink team's Cobra first, expending all of its ordinance on the complex. Next the Max section worked on the complex. On the 11th or 12th run the minigun on one of the Cobras malfunctioned and fired 6 rounds which landed in and around the small Ranger perimeter. One round struck Pacheco in the back and exited through the chest region, causing a sucking chest wound. The Team Leader told the pink team commander he needed to get him out as soon as possible, while the team members stopped his sucking chest wound with a five quart canteen. Two members of the team carried him to the nearest semblance of an LZ, and the pink team's low bird came in, taking several blade strikes in the process. Although he was barely alive when placed on the low bird, he expired while on the chopper and was dead when it landed at Spudis.

The company felt a great loss upon Pacheco's death. He was a deeply religious man and so well liked that it seems so cruel that he should die in such a fluke. A memorial service was held in his honor and each member of the command gave him his last salute. I can honestly say that he is one of the few in this world who had no enemies.

I thank you on behalf of all Rangers for the stories you wrote about us, and assure you that many copies of the Garry Owen were sent home to friends and relatives. If I can be of further assistance, do not hesitate to contact me.
Sincerely,
/s/
JOHN A. FENILI

1st LETTER FROM JAIME:

16-April-72

Dear Doug,

It was sure good to hear from you my fellow Brother IN our Lord Jesus Christ. Yes I did get the books and the very Beautiful bible you sent me. Thank you. I can tell you already I have put it to use and rest assured it <u>will</u> see more use.

I would sure loved to hear your sermon that you preached that Sunday night. It seems our Lord has a place for you in the ministry seeing as you loved it. I don't know what our good Lord has for me but I tell you when he leads or shows me to where he wants me I'll know I can't ever be happy unless I do as he wants me too. As for my going home, I don't know yet. I'll just let Him take care of that as he has taken care of me in All things. Doug I just can't thank you enough for what you have done for me if there is anything I can do for you here let me know and I'll be more than glad to do it for you.

Those books you sent me are Outstanding. I liked them very much especially <u>God's Smuggler</u> by Brother (In Christ) Andrew.

As for any duration missions I haven't pulled any since you left. Just after you left we went out (Team 76) and on the second day early in the morning we made contact. 1 enemy KIA and 1 POW. The KIA was between the T.L. and me. The POW was taken by me when we went to check out the kill zone and strip the bodies. You know if it had been some else other than me at the point they would of killed that man. I thank God I was there and with Christ in my heart leading me I seen that he didn't have any fight left (in the enemy soldier). It just something I seen in his eyes when he opened them and met mine. I understood that if I hade of killed, which could have easily been done, I would never be able to rest in peace again. That is why I give thanks to God for Him leading me the Right Way. But if the enemy soldier had of made a move to his wheapon or seemed like he had a grenade I wouldn't of hesitated to kill him. But as you see Our Lord took care of All of it.

As you know Doug things are getting bad over here and just recently we started 3 man tank killer teams. I am in one of them as of yet we haven't gone out but the way things are going it might be soon. So I ask you to remember us in your prayers and ask other people to do the same for us. It would greatly be appreciated.

Well Doug, I guess this is about all I've got to say for now and I'll pray for you. So may God Bless us All through Christ Jesus <u>our</u> Lord.

P.S. How are you and your Girl doing? Any plans? Let me know and I know if it be our Lords will to go back to the States alive and well,
We, my family and I will meet again someday.

Take care Doug
Give my regards to your folks.
Your fellow
<u>Brother</u> in Christ
Jaime Pacheco

LETTER FROM JAIME

Hello Doug,

Old friend I am truly sorry I took this long to answer your most welcome letter. I have been on radio relay and I haven't been back in the rear for a while. I'll be going out to the field in a couple of days so I am making the most of the free time I have. One thing you don't have to worry about is that we have discontinued the "Tank Killer" teams for the time being but we are keeping our "LAWs" handy.

As for any news around here as far as action goes things have been a little slack (especially me) but there's been a couple of teams make contact, find caches and a few kills and such. But one thing I have found out, and that is that I'll be here a while (Mission esential). Also my drop hasn't come down and there is a posibility that I could serve a whole year in Nam. Man let me tell you something, I am ready to go home right now! Personally I would like I said go home right now but if I had my way I would like to go the 18th of June so I could be there for her birthday and after all out processing arrive at my home town the morning of the 20th of June. But the way things look it seems that it will be more like in August or the very latest October (1 year). At any rate if it goes to the worst, as of now I am caught up financially on all my bills and debts paid off and have saved up (te-te-) so all the rest of the money I am making here goes to keep up the bills we have and the rest into savings.

So it all turns out just fine. But I still would like to be home. But at any rate I am going to let God lead me and use me according to His <u>will</u>. Yes that is the way to be

<u>Doug, God **IS** GOOD.</u>

Hey you asked me if I am in touch with the guys you sang with over here, yes I still see them. Steve is still here so is Hank but I can't remember his name. He used to be Special Forces. He Derosed a few days ago and I said Hello to them in your name.

Say <u>Brother</u>—I see you tell me that you preached at Kalispell and it seems that you are getting involved with the young people and starting up a group (I hope?)

I also got you phone number and I will give you a call when I get home and I will invite you for <u>THE</u> <u>Best</u> Mexican food you have ever ate and will ever eat. A Big Brag but it can be <u>kept!</u>

I'll be waiting to hear from you so in the mean time you'll be in my prayers and thoughts. Amigo asta Leugo

In CHRIST
FOR ETERNITY
Your <u>Brother</u>
Jaime Pacheco

LETTER FROM OLGA PACHECO

July 1, 1972
Sunday

We seem to give them
Back to Thee, O God,
Who gavest them to us.

Dear Mr. Sterner,

How difficult it is to write a letter when you want it to be filled with sincere gratitude and appreciation. I found your letter to be most consoling, and I must thank you for uniting yourself with us in our hour of grief over the loss of our beloved Jaime. Yes, "God is Good", He has been very good to me, and with His grace I have felt and experienced strength in this time of anguish.

Realizing how you cherish the friendship you and my dear husband shared, I must ask you to please keep the letters you so generously offered to give to me, but I would like to have the pictures you mentioned in your letter. I am also very interested in getting some copies of the book you have just completed. And I am sure Jaime would consider it a high honor if you were to dedicate this book to him.

I will save both your letters and when our son, Michael, who is now eighteen months old, is big enough to understand and appreciate the wonderful father he had, I will proudly have him read them.

Mr. Sterner, you seem to be a man full of Christian love for your fellow man, won't you please keep Michael and I in your prayers? It is my wish and prayer that the "Good God" continue helping me face my future with a smile, a smile at God in loving acceptance of whatever He sends into my life now, so that I may merit to have the radiant, smiling face of Christ gaze on me for all eternity.

Gratefully in Jesus Christ
(Mrs.) Olga Pacheco

LEFT: During an August 2000 visit to Michael at his home in Texas, I was finally privileged to meet Olga, Jaime's widow.

30

EPILOGUE

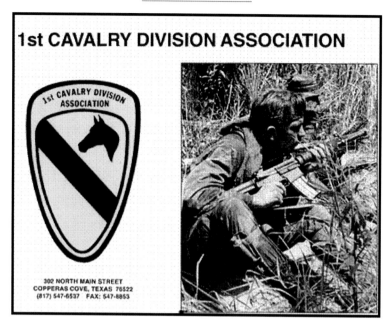

1st CAVALRY DIVISION ASSOCIATION

1st CAVALRY DIVISION
ASSOCIATION

302 NORTH MAIN STREET
COPPERAS COVE, TEXAS 76522
(817) 547-6537   FAX: 547-8853

Jaime's story sometimes seems to me to be a story that, each time I begin to believe has reached a conclusion, generates a new chapter. For many years I was stunned by the "fluke accident" that cost my best friend his life. As time goes by, I realize more and more than somehow in God's own Master Plan, there are no fluke accidents...that everything happens for a reason, and that "All things work together for good" (Romans 8:28).

After my Memorial Day 1998 meeting with Jaime's family, Michael emailed me and asked if I would submit Jaime's Story to one of the websites that told the stories of America's veterans. I did so, and when I did not get any quick responses, decided to try and create a website for the story myself. (I was a computer novice but just six months earlier had returned to our local community college to study computers).

Jaime's Story was my first effort at web authoring, and the story went online on a free homepage server on Father's Day of 1998. That first effort became both an inspiration and motivation to do more online, and the following month I posted the first pages in my HomeOfHeroes.com website. In the years that followed it became one of the largest (currently over 50,000 printed pages) and most visited (10 million hits each month at present) websites on the Internet. As I recently pointed out to Michael, thirty years after his father's death in Vietnam, Jaime continues to impact the lives of thousands of people each month.

Two years after I posted Jaime's Story on the Internet, I visited the site one day to see the following entry in the guestbook:

That same year (2000) Michael, Lenay and Tyler spent a week with our family in Pueblo to attend the Medal of Honor Society convention, which was being held here. Over the years as Pam and I have been highly involved with our friends who wear our Nation's highest military honor, we have spoken often of Jaime, for he is the source of our motivation. During that week many of the recipients, all of whom knew Jaime's story and many of whom had copies of the calendar bearing Jaime's and my picture, expressed their appreciation to Michael for the sacrifices of his family. During the same week Michael celebrated a birthday and we were privileged to throw a party for him. It was the first birthday in his young life that he had celebrated with a *father*.

The same year I received an email from a young lady whose father had recently passed away. She told me her father had been the Team Leader for Ranger Team 74 on the day Jaime was killed. Her father had recently passed away and in her grieving she had begun to try to learn more about him. Her father, she told me, had spoken all his life about a fellow ranger named Jaime Pacheco who had saved his life. In her quest she found Jaime's Story on the internet and became yet one more of the thousands of Americans whose lives have been touched and inspired by the life and death of Jaime Pacheco.

Michael Pacheco (Center) with MOH Recipients in 2000

Today Michael, Lenay and Tyler are an important part of the Sterner family, and for all intents and purposes, I claim them as my own kids. My one regret is that I didn't meet Michael earlier; that I never had the opportunity to be there for him in his youth.

On the last weekend of June 2002 I was asked to attend the first ever reunion of the Pacheco-Vejar family. For me it was an opportunity to keep a 30 year old promise to travel to Hobbs, New Mexico and meet Jaime's family. That weekend I was introduced as "the guest of honor", but I was treated like a very close member of the Pacheco-Vejar family.

Top Left: Doug with Jaime's brothers Robert and Alfred. **Bottom Left:** Doug with Jaime's sister Lilly. **Right:** Doug and Pam, Michael and Lenay with *Mom Pacheco.*

During that wonderful and emotional weekend in Hobbs, at last I fulfilled my dream of one day visiting Jaime's grave site. Instead of meeting Jaime's family as I stood at his grave, however, when the dream at last came true I went there with his son and grandson. Together we decorated the final resting place of a man we all admired while reassuring ourselves that we would remain united in our love and commitment to each other, and never forget the lesson we learned from Jaime....

God Is Good!

If in fact, there is a final chapter to Jaime's story, perhaps it came during that family reunion in Hobbs. As mentioned in the preface to this booklet, over the years the only mementos of my Vietnam service that survived were the letters from or regarding Jaime and my black beret. Shortly after finding Michael I sent him the originals of the letters. When we first met at Angel Fire I showed him the beret and said, "This too, is yours if you ask for it...but please don't ask."

Michael smiled knowingly and said, "No Doug, that belongs to you."

For 30 years, though faded and worn, that beret has sat prominently on the mantle in my office, a continuing reminder of why I do the many things I do.

As I prepared for the family reunion in Hobbs, a new realization began to nag at my conscience. I knew Jaime's family wanted me to speak at their reunion, and deep inside I knew that there was yet one more thing I needed to do to come full-circle with my memories of Jaime.

Traveling to Hobbs I had a plan. Unsure I could actually do it until the last minute, I hadn't even consulted Pam, so it surprised ever her. At the

conclusion of my words to Jaime's family I asked Tyler to join me at the front of the room, removed the black beret that I had worn only for special moments over the years, and placed it on his head.

Today in its place on my mantle is a photograph, for though we can never forget those we have loved and lost, we must always remember that life is for the living. God has given me something far more important that that beret to remind me of my friendship with Jaime. He has given me a wonderful family.

Jaime's Awards

Silver Star
Bronze Star with "V" and 2 OLC*
Air Medal
Army Commendation Medal "V" and OLC*
Purple Heart
National Defense Service Medal
Vietnam Service Medal
Vietnam Cross of Gallantry
Vietnam Campaign Medal
Combat Infantryman Badge
Parachutist Bade
Pathfinder Badge
Sharpshooter Badge with Automatic Rifle

*OLC (Oak Leaf Cluster) – indicates additional awards of the same medal. The Bronze Star with 2 OLC indicates three awards of this medal. The "V" indicates that the award was earned for heroic actions.

Made in the USA
Columbia, SC
17 May 2020